District Deputy's Guide

INDEPENDENT ORDER OF ODD FELLOWS

MICHAEL GREENZEIGER

HEART IN HAND INSTITUTE

Second Edition: May 2024

Illustrations by Ainslie Heilich

Preface by Toby Hanson

ISBN 978-1-962553-01-0

ACKNOWLEDGEMENTS

Thank you to Sister Debra LaVergne, President of the Rebekah Assembly of California, for her assistance in preparing the Second Edition of this work to include District Deputy Presidents in addition to District Deputy Grand Masters.

CONTENTS

PREFACE

In between the local lodge and the Grand Lodge or Rebekah Assembly of each jurisdiction exists a critical link—the District Deputy Grand Master or District Deputy President. District Deputies are the eyes and ears of the Grand Master or Assembly President and are able to observe operations of local lodges and help keep them functioning at their best. Even the most ambitious leader is often not able to visit each lodge in their jurisdiction, especially in the larger jurisdictions. They rely on their deputies in each district to observe the lodges and report on them. Deputies can help identify and solve problems before they arise and cause greater disruption. A well-trained and knowledgeable District Deputy is a critical part of a functional jurisdiction.

As membership in our Order declined in the 20th Century, the job of District Deputy has often been a victim of benign neglect. Too often the job has gone unfilled or untrained. Brother Michael Greenzeiger, PGM of California, discovered as much in 2018 when he served as Grand Instructor. In his travels around the state organizing educational opportunities for District Deputies, he discovered that over many previous years the education and training of those Deputies had fallen by the wayside. The discovery of the lack of training and knowledge prompted Brother Greenzeiger to write the original DDGM Training Manual for California, from which his later project, The Odd Fellows' Primer, sprang forth. Despite the universal praise for the Primer and its widespread adoption, there still exists a specialized need for education and training for the District Deputies of our Order.

To that end, Brother Greenzeiger has updated and adapted his original California text to make it as broadly applicable as possible. Given the diversity of jurisdictional rules across the worldwide fraternity of Odd Fellowship, it's impossible to have a truly complete and comprehensive work. However, this Guide should be sufficient for the vast majority of cases. It is the sincere hope and wish of the author and all who have contributed to this project that it will first and foremost enrich those who perform the job of District Deputy. All of us have a strong belief in the value of Odd Fellowship and strive to share our knowledge, skills, and experience to improve Odd Fellowship. We hope that Grand Lodges and Rebekah Assemblies all across the globe will find value in this text and use it as a primary or supplementary source material when training their Deputies.

The highest compliment any of us who have worked on this text could hope for is that it become a valued part of spreading the knowledge of Odd Fellowship. District Deputies, when properly trained, can be an invaluable asset to jurisdictional leaders and form a strong central link in the chain binding local lodges to their respective jurisdictional bodies. With this training Guide available, hopefully Grand Lodges and Rebekah Assemblies will be able to avoid spending time and resources developing their own materials for training Deputies and focus more on deploying those Deputies to assist the lodges in their jurisdictions. It is our sincere hope that this text becomes a valued part of District Deputy training throughout Odd Fellowship. As a Past Grand Master myself, I can personally attest to the importance of a functioning system of District Deputies. My District Deputies were a critical part of the success of my term and I hope that other jurisdictions will have similar success as a result of using this Guide for their District.

In Friendship, Love, and Truth,
Toby Hanson, Past Grand Master
Grand Lodge of Washington, IOOF

1

INTRODUCTION

Welcome to one of the most important positions in our Order. For many of you this will not be the first time you have served in this office. No matter how many times one has served, however, there is always more to learn and room for improvement. The District Deputy Grand Master (DDGM) and District Deputy President (DDP) serve as the connection point between the lodges of their district and the Grand Master or Rebekah Assembly President respectively. For some lodges, the District Deputy will be their main contact with the Ritual, laws, and traditions of the Order.

The position encompasses a wide variety of roles: teacher, mediator, legal arbiter, supporter, and friend. No one person is likely to enjoy or excel at all these aspects, but we must do our best to be proficient in each of them. A part in the success of your lodges, Noble Grands, and other officers rests on your shoulders. Your Grand Instructor, if you have one in your jurisdiction, stands ready to help you achieve success in any way that they can. Your Grand Master and other Grand Lodge officers are also there to lend a hand. By working together you can make it a great year for Odd Fellowship in your district.

This book is not a replacement for your Grand Master, or the laws and customs of your particular jurisdiction. These should always be given priority and adhered to.

2

QUALIFICATIONS AND DUTIES

Qualifications

You are qualified to be a DDGM or DDP by virtue of being a member in good standing within the Grand Lodge or Rebekah Assembly respectively. Being a member of Grand Lodge requires being Past Grand of an Odd Fellows Lodge and being a member in good standing of an Odd Fellows Lodge in good standing. Being a member of Rebekah Assembly requires being Past Noble Grand of a Rebekah Lodge or Past Grand of an Odd Fellows Lodge and a member in good standing of a Rebekah Lodge in good standing.

You have been recommended by your lodge, endorsed by the other lodges in district, if applicable, and appointed by the Grand Master or Assembly President. You are known to be an experienced Odd Fellow or Rebekah with knowledge and wisdom to share with the lodges of your district. You are ready and willing to serve the Order and to extend your hand in friendship beyond those members of the Order you regularly associate with. If a DDGM, you must prove yourself in the Unwritten Work of the Initiatory Degree and the Three Degrees before receiving your commission and assuming your position. If a DDP, you must prove yourself in the Unwritten Work of the Rebekah Degree and the charges of the District Deputy President in the Installation Ceremony. Even if your district only performs Joint Installations, you will need to be able to administer the Obligation to the Elective Officers.

Duties and Expectations

Appoint a Staff

In order to fulfill your responsibility as DDGM or DDP to perform official visits and installations you will need a staff to assist you.

Your staff must all be Past Grands or Past Noble Grands from lodges in your district. It is ideal to select individuals from around the entire district to spread out the work and to give everyone a chance at leadership positions. It is particularly useful to include newer Past Grands or Past Noble Grands on your staff so that they can become more involved around your district.

The first officer you will want to choose is your District Deputy Grand Marshal (Odd Fellow) or District Deputy Marshal (Rebekah). They will ideally be accompanying you on all your official visits.

Filling all of the positions listed in the installation ceremony is a good idea, and will help you to perform the ceremony credibly.

When appointing district officer positions, be mindful of the offices that individuals might hold in their local lodges. For example, avoid appointing someone who is Secretary of their local lodge to be District Deputy Grand Secretary (Odd Fellow) or District Deputy Secretary (Rebekah). This will avoid the awkward situation of a person having to install themselves, or of having to shuffle your staff at the last minute.

Visitations

You are to make at least two official visits to each lodge in your district. The first visit should be as soon as is practical after your installation. At that first visit, be sure to present your commission and inform the lodges in your district about the Grand Master's or Assembly President's programs. The second visit is generally after the new officers have been installed and may include instruction and training for the newly installed officers.

By spacing your official visits out in this manner you will have the opportunity to visit the lodge when each of the two different set of individuals who hold office during your term are presiding.

During your visitations you will be expected to speak last, so you may wish to prepare a written speech if you don't feel comfortable speaking extemporaneously.

In addition to speaking on the Grand Master's or Assembly President's programs and upcoming activities in the district or state, it can also be valuable to speak about the meaning of Odd Fellowship and about our symbols and traditions.

When you speak at a lodge, it is generally a good idea to compliment the lodge and its officers on what they have done particularly well. Your duty also includes guiding lodges and members on what they may not be doing correctly. However, this information is better delivered privately, rather than in front of the entire lodge.

Spending time socializing and getting to know the lodge members during your visit is also very helpful to building the spirit of fraternity within your lodges.

Annual Term Reports

Before a lodge can hold their annual installation of officers, they must first complete their annual report and submit it to the Grand Lodge or Rebekah Assembly along with all funds due. The lodge may send it directly to the Grand Lodge or Rebekah Assembly office or place it directly in your hands, but must make the report available for your review in either case. You should read it over to verify that it is in order before proceeding with the installation.

Installations

Installations are typically performed in January. A lodge is not eligible to be installed before they have submitted the previous year's term report. Be sure to arrange the date for the installation with each lodge well in advance and notify your installation team so they will all be available and ready to assist you.

You should also check with each lodge to learn what type of installation they would like you to perform. The closed form of the installation, which can be found in the standard <u>Charge Book for an Odd Fellows Lodge</u> or <u>Charge Book for a Rebekah Lodge</u>, is appropriate if the lodge will have no outside guests. This, however, is rarely the case. If friends and family will be attending, you should use the public version of this ritual.

When an Odd Fellows Lodge combines with a Rebekah Lodge for installation, the ceremony to use is the "Joint Public Installation." You can find this ritual in the District Deputy kit, suitcase, or other materials you will be receiving from your predecessor. Be sure to coordinate with your counterpart in the Odd Fellows or Rebekahs to ensure a smooth joint installation. It's a good idea to rehearse a bit with the installing officers to ensure everyone is comfortable with the installation ritual.

For those lodges who prefer more informal ceremony, have limited space available, have members with mobility issues, or who simply enjoy having lodge dinners, the "Dinner Installation" may be the best option. This may also be found in your District Deputy materials or acquired from your Grand Lodge or Rebekah Assembly.

<u>District Meetings</u>

One of the biggest advantages of belonging to a lodge organization such as ours is the opportunity to interact with high quality people beyond one's own local lodge. In many districts, district-wide meetings are held at least once a year in order to coordinate between the lodges of the district and facilitate cooperation and participation in each other's events.

If you've never been to one, find out how district meetings are organized in your district. It may just be that the Noble Grands and Vice Grands of the local lodges are invited, or perhaps other officers as well. In some cases, a district meeting is open to any member in good standing of a lodge in the district. If there are no district meetings in your district, you may wish to consider starting one.

Typically, a district meeting will be scheduled and lead by the DDGM or DDP. Some use district meetings to sync up the calendar for the coming year so that all the lodges are able to attend each other's events. There may also be other matters to discuss such as working together on initiations, service events, or social events. Having a close-knit district can be a huge boon to lodges, especially the smaller ones who might not be able to hold elaborate events without the cooperation of other lodges.

Schools of Instruction

Holding a School of Instruction for your district is a great way to help educate the members of your lodges about Odd Fellowship. Our tradition is very deep so there is always something new for a member to learn. The DDGM and DDP may work together to put one on for both Odd Fellows and Rebekahs. If desired, a few districts may even combine for a larger event.

You should tailor the subject matter to the interests of the members in your district. Some may be interested in understanding the meaning of our ceremonies, symbols, and philosophy. Others may want to know more what charitable causes and what service opportunities our Order offers. Still others may want to learn more about what types of events they can hold to better attract new members. It is also very important to make sure the teaching is at a level appropriate for the audience. You may be dealing with new members, 50-year members, or a combination of everything in between.

While you should take the lead in planning a School of Instruction for your district, you don't need to do all the teaching yourself. You may invite any knowledgeable member to assist with the teaching and you may also contact the Grand Instructor, if applicable, to invite them to assist you in locating appropriate speakers for your event.

Interpret the Laws of the Order

In the course of your term of office, you may be called upon to issue a ruling on a point of Odd Fellow or Rebekah law. The Noble Grand is the highest authority in a local lodge, but their ruling may be appealed to you.

If you are asked to make a ruling, you must use the written laws of the Order as your guide. If you do not immediately know the answer, it is better to admit that you aren't sure and take the time to read the applicable laws before issuing a ruling.

No one knows all the laws from memory, but you can know where to find the information you need to make a legal and just ruling. The law may not be clear on a particular point and in those cases you should be prepared to exercise your own judgement based on your understanding of the letter and the spirit of the law.

You are obligated to submit all rulings you make to the Grand Master or Assembly President in writing. Your ruling on a particular matter will stand unless they choose to overturn your ruling. If the Grand Master or Assembly President has already spoken on a particular issue, their ruling must be enforced.

Grant Dispensations

The laws of your Jurisdiction provide for certain specific dispensations you are permitted to bestow upon lodges in your district. You should check in your Grand Lodge's or Rebekah Assembly's Constitution and By-Laws for a definitive list which may include some or all of the following:

- To confer multiple degrees on the same day

- To hold public installations of officers

- To install Third Degree members as Vice Grand or Noble Grand who do not have previous service in the required number of offices, provided all qualified brothers or sisters decline to serve

- To allow brothers or sisters to appear in public in regalia

No dispensation may be given which is not provided for in the legal codes operative within your Jurisdiction.

Represent the Grand Master or Assembly President

When the Grand Master or Assembly President is not present, you are their representative within your district. This is why you receive the Honors of the Order on your official visits, a privilege that would otherwise be reserved for the Grand Master or Assembly President and other elected jurisdictional officers. Therefore, when you receive the Honors you should be sure to thank the lodge on behalf of the Grand Master or Assembly President. You may not receive them when that officer is present.

As the Grand Master's or Assembly President's representative, the manner in which you conduct yourself is a reflection on that officer. You should always make the best possible impression by dressing nicely, practicing your role in the Ritual and otherwise so that you may fulfill it competently, and always treating others with kindness and respect.

You are also to support and publicize the programs of the Grand Master or Assembly President within your district. Not every Odd Fellow or Rebekah has a chance to meet these officers directly or to hear them speak, so you will be their point of contact with the Grand Master's or Assembly President's programs. Be sure to familiarize yourself with those programs so that you may share your knowledge with Odd Fellows and Rebekahs around your district.

Attend Official Visits of the Grand Master or Assembly President

The Grand Master or Assembly President will most likely visit at least one lodge in your district during your term. As DDGM or DDP, it is your responsibility to attend that visit. You must support the Grand Master or Assembly President and act as Marshal if none of their other officers are present and able to perform in that capacity.

You are expected to attend if any other representative of the Grand Master or Assembly President visits your district, such as the Deputy Grand Master or Assembly Vice President. Attending official visits in nearby districts is also recommended.

Should you act as Marshal, it will be your responsibility to line up the dignitaries in the anteroom prior to escort. Always remember that the most important person being escorted enters last. If it is a Rebekah Lodge meeting, the Rebekah Assembly officers take precedence whereas if it is an Odd Fellows Lodge meeting, the Grand Lodge officers take precedence.

For Past Elective Officers, the order of escort is:

1. Grand Junior Lodge and Theta Rho Assembly

2. Department Council of Patriarchs Militant and Department Association of Ladies Auxiliary Patriarchs Militant (LAPM)

3. Grand Encampment and Grand Ladies Encampment Auxiliary

4. Grand Lodge and Rebekah Assembly

5. Sovereign Grand Lodge, International Association of Rebekah Assemblies, General Military Council, and International Association Ladies Auxiliaries of the Patriarchs Militant

For current Elective Officers, the order of escort is:

1. Grand Junior Lodge and Theta Rho Assembly

2. Department Council of Patriarchs Militant

3. Grand Encampment and Grand Ladies Encampment Auxiliary

4. Grand Lodge and Rebekah Assembly

Current Elective Officers of Sovereign Grand Lodge, International Association of Rebekah Assemblies, and General Military Council of the Patriarchs Militant will often be escorted separately after the above groups are done.

See that Ritual Work is Proficient

The ritualistic work of our Order is a big part of what defines us as Odd Fellows and Rebekahs. It contains the meaning of who we are and what we do. You are charged to ensure that ritualistic work in your district is performed in a proficient and dignified manner. Not everyone is able to learn a part from memory, but everyone can at least get better at performing that part with practice, even if they have to read from a book.

While you cannot expect perfection, the important thing is that you foster a culture wherein the ritual work of the Order is taken seriously and performed with effort and care. If we don't act as though the work of Odd Fellowship matters to us, then we should not expect it to matter to our new members. If Odd Fellowship doesn't matter, why should anyone join or participate?

Report Violations of Law by Lodges

All Odd Fellows are bound to obey the laws of the Order so long as they do not conflict with the laws of the land or their moral duty. Part of your role is to be the eyes and ears of the Grand Master or Assembly President in your district and alert them to any violations of the laws, rules, and regulations of the Order by the lodges in your charge. This includes any violation of lawful commands you may issue as part of your responsibilities as DDGM or DDP. You will receive contact information for the Grand Master or Assembly President and should not hesitate to use it if a situation arises in which you feel the laws of our Order have been violated.

Make a Final Report

Your final duty is to render a final written report to the Grand Master or Assembly President. In this report you should include a summary of your activities, including visitations made, installations performed, decisions rendered, dispensations granted and any other activities you have performed for the benefit of your district. You should also include a statement of the condition of each lodge in your charge as well as any recommendations you may have for the well-being of the Order in your district, your jurisdiction, and beyond.

Typically, Grand Masters and Assembly Presidents prefer to receive reports from their DDGMs or DDPs sufficiently before the end of the term to allow for the incorporation of feedback from the Deputies into the Grand Master's or Assembly President's own final report. Depending on the jurisdiction and the officer, there may also be requirements to report periodically during the course of the year. Some jurisdictions provide pre-prepared forms for DDGM or DDP reports while others expect reports to be completed free-form.

3

ABOUT ODD FELLOWSHIP

Principles and Purpose

One of questions you will most frequently be asked by members and non-members alike is "What is the purpose of Odd Fellowship?"

The answer you give may well determine if an individual chooses to associate with our Order or to continue said membership. People want to know why we do what we do and what it means to us.

There is no precise right or wrong answer to be given for questions like these because the nature of every lodge and indeed every Odd Fellow and Rebekah is different. Nevertheless, a few key principles have persisted over time throughout our Order's long and storied history.

As is taught in our Ritual, Odd Fellowship is about having a place where we can meet as brothers and sisters on equal footing and without the "masks" we often wear to keep each other from knowing us as our truest selves. A person's station in life doesn't matter in the lodge room and nor should our petty likes and dislikes. We are bound together as children of one common Parent and thus obligated to help and support each other through the trials and travails of life.

Our purpose in coming together is to elevate the world as a whole, to make it a better place in which all human beings are bound together in brotherly and sisterly love. Such a world would be a paradise and we can do our part simply by exercising the principles of Friendship, Love, and Truth in all our interactions within the lodge room as well as in the outside world.

Beyond our core principles, there are infinite possibilities for how a lodge can be. One may think of it as a platform for holding whatever social, fraternal, or service activities fit the desires and interests of its members – so long as those activities are in harmony with our principles.

Lodges have been successful in many different ways: through shared meals and parties, sponsoring and organizing activities, sharing in hobbies, serving the local community in whatever capacity, raising money to give to good causes, practicing and performing the Ritual of the Order, studying the deeper meanings of Odd Fellowship and its symbols, or engaging with our history. What is important is that each lodge finds its own way to be which works for its members and their community, and adds to the overall vibrancy of our worldwide Order.

Structure and Governance

Local Lodges

The most important body in Odd Fellowship is a local lodge. The local lodge is the only body which can perform the degree work necessary to initiate a new Odd Fellow or Rebekah. It is also the main point of contact that both our members and the general public have with our Order. Most of the day-to-day decisions within our Order happen within the domain of a local lodge. The strength of our local lodges is the main thing which will determine our future.

A local lodge is governed by a set of elected and appointed officers who fulfill both functional and ceremonial roles.

The highest officer in both an Odd Fellow and Rebekah Lodge is the Noble Grand who chairs the meetings, appoints most committees, and generally sets the agenda for the year.

The Vice Grand chairs meetings in the absence of the Noble Grand, has charge of the Inner Door, and may be assigned additional responsibilities in some lodges, such as organizing refreshments.

A local lodge also elects a Secretary, a Financial Secretary, and a Treasurer (though some lodges combine the functions of the Secretary and the Financial Secretary). These officers collectively have responsibility for the record keeping of the lodge with the Secretary focusing on minutes and correspondence, the Financial Secretary handling dues collection and other income, and the Treasurer overseeing disbursements.

Many lodges elect Trustees to be responsible for managing the investments or assets of the lodge and maintaining the physical condition of the building and any other property owned by the lodge, such as commercial storefronts or cemeteries.

The Noble Grand in an Odd Fellow Lodge appoints a series of "line" officers with primarily ceremonial function: the Warden, Conductor, Right Scene Supporter, Left Scene Supporter, Inside Guardian, and Outside Guardian. These officers form a line in the sense that one would traditionally start as Outside Guardian and move one's way up the line until eventually after being Warden an individual would be elected Vice Grand and then Noble Grand. This way a member gets to learn the various functions of the lodge officers and work their way through increasing responsibilities before running the lodge.

Rebekah Lodges have similar line officers with the exception that there are no Scene Supporters. Part and parcel of the progressive line system is the notion that the leadership of a lodge should change every year and that as many members as possible should be given the opportunity to lead. Some lodges may not be able to fill all of the line officer positions. Other lodges may only have older, more experienced members who have been through the line many times. Regardless, the goal of developing new members and equitably sharing the responsibilities in the lodge is a worthy one.

There are also several other positions which are appointed by the Noble Grand or Vice Grand and fulfill a variety of functions for the lodge, such as the Chaplain who presides over benedictions, the Musician who provides musical accompaniment, and the Supporters of the Noble Grand and Vice Grand who are generally experienced past presiding officers capable of advising and teaching the present Noble Grand and Vice Grand about their duties. In an Odd Fellows Lodge the lodge is opened and closed by the Right Supporter of the Noble Grand, but in a Rebekah Lodge this function is performed by the Warden.

The District

The lodges within a geographical vicinity are combined to form a district, which can vary in both geographic size and number of lodges. The district exists for the purpose of fostering cooperation and fraternal relations between Odd Fellows and Rebekahs in different lodges. It also provides a convenient way to help disseminate information and guidance from the Grand Lodge and Grand Master or from the Rebekah Assembly and Assembly President to the local lodges.

The district is lead by a District Deputy Grand Master (DDGM) or District Deputy President (DDP) who is appointed by the Grand Master or Assembly President upon the recommendation of one or more lodges in the district. Many districts have an arrangement wherein each lodge gets to take a turn in recommending the DDGM or DDP for the following year. The DDGM or DDP is responsible for appointing the other district officers.

In some districts, in addition to their role in performing installations and other ritual functions, the district officers have other responsibilities as well. Some districts have district funds that can be used for the needs of the district and may also have district level committees to further the work of the Order on a district level.

Grand Bodies

Grand Lodges are composed of all Past Grands in good standing of the Odd Fellow Lodges in the jurisdiction, who have received the Grand Lodge Degree. Rebekah Assemblies are composed of all Rebekah members in good standing who have received the Rebekah Assembly Degree. These include Past Noble Grands of Rebekah Lodges and Past Grands of Odd Fellow Lodges.

Grand Lodges and Rebekah Assemblies exist for the purpose of promoting the aims of Odd Fellowship throughout their jurisdiction as well as having a supervisory role over the local lodges. Promoting the aims of Odd Fellowship can take many forms and encompasses both promoting Odd Fellowship to the general public as well as promoting the principles and traditions of Odd Fellowship within the Order.

Each Odd Fellows Lodge elects Representatives to their Grand Lodge from amongst its Past Grands. Rebekah Lodges elect Representatives from its members who are Past Noble Grands or Past Grands. These representatives are empowered to cast votes on matters that come before the Grand

Lodge or Rebekah Assembly in accordance with the will of their lodge. The number of allocated representatives is dependent on the size of the local lodge and the laws of the jurisdiction.

Grand Lodges and Rebekah Assemblies meet once a year in regular session to vote on bills and resolutions which come before them for purposes of amending the laws of the Grand Lodge or Rebekah Assembly, or deciding upon what course of action to take on issues. Grand Lodges and Rebekah Assemblies also elect their officers at the annual session. Additionally, special sessions may be called during the year, particularly if there is business that requires immediate action, though this is rare in most jurisdictions.

The top officer in a Grand Lodge is the Grand Master who has charge of all ritualistic functions within the jurisdiction, appoints officers and committees, and presents a program for benefit of Odd Fellowship in the jurisdiction during his or her year. The Grand Master is assisted by the Deputy Grand Master and Grand Warden who are elected in a progressive line similar to the one used in a local lodge. Similarly, the top officer in a Rebekah Assembly is the Assembly President who is assisted by the Vice President and Warden.

Other elected officers include the Grand Secretary or Assembly Secretary and Grand Treasurer or Assembly Treasurer who fulfill recording keeping and financial functions similar to those officers in a local lodge. Additionally, Grand Lodges elect one or two Grand Representatives, depending on the size of the jurisdiction, who represent the Grand Lodge in sessions of The Sovereign Grand Lodge. Rebekah Assemblies elect one Representative to the International Association of Rebekah Assemblies, which is subordinate to the Sovereign Grand Lodge. There may be other elected officers as well, depending on the jurisdiction.

The appointed officers of the Grand Lodge and Rebekah Assembly fulfill primarily ceremonial functions that are parallel to the appointed officers of a local lodge. There may also be additional appointed officers with other roles, such as a Grand Instructor who has a primarily teaching function.

As Grand Lodges and Rebekah Assemblies are generally only in session for a few days each year, they have an Executive Committee (or Board of Directors, depending on the jurisdiction) composed of elected officers to make necessary decisions in the interim. Executive Committees and Boards are not permitted to exercise any of the legislative functions of the Grand Lodge or Rebekah Assembly.

The Sovereign Grand Lodge

The Sovereign Grand Lodge (SGL) is the highest authority in the Independent Order of Odd Fellows worldwide. It is composed of the Grand Representatives from among the various jurisdictions and also meets annually for purposes of passing bills and resolutions and electing its own officers. The SGL has sole authority over the Ritual of the Order, including all the degree rituals. It also has ultimate authority over the appendant bodies of the Order, such as the Encampment and Patriarchs Militant. The SGL has a structure similar to Grand Lodge with the highest officer being the Sovereign Grand Master and further elected and appointed officers corresponding to most of those of a Grand Lodge.

The International Association of Rebekah Assemblies

The International Association of Rebekah Assemblies (IARA) is the top international Rebekah body, though is itself subordinate to Sovereign

Grand Lodge. Similar to SGL, it is composed of Representatives, though only one is allowed per jurisdiction regardless of size. It also elects its own officers and passes legislation, but its bills must be reviewed by the SGL prior to taking effect. The IARA is allocated a Grand Representative to represent its interests at SGL. Its structure reflects that of a Rebekah Assembly with the highest officer being the International President and further elected and appointed officers corresponding to those of a Rebekah Assembly.

The Laws of the Order

The Laws of the Order are contained in a variety of different documents on an international, jurisdictional, and local lodge level. It is entirely possible that these documents may come to contradict each other and when they do it is important to know the order of precedence our different sources of law take.

The ultimate authority in Odd Fellowship is to be found in the Ritual. If any of other laws are not in accordance with those written in the Charge Books or other sources of Ritual, we are obligated to follow the Ritual. Next we are to follow The Sovereign Grand Lodge's Code of General Laws and afterwards, the Constitution, By-Laws, and Standing Rules of the Grand Lodge or Rebekah Assembly in that order. Finally we are to obey the Constitution, By-Laws, and Standing Rules of our local lodge. In cases of parliamentary procedure, where each of these sources of law remain silent, we are to follow the current edition of Robert's Rules of Order, Newly Revised.

If interpretation is necessary, the decision is to be made by the Noble Grand of the lodge but may subsequently be appealed to the District Deputy Grand Master or District Deputy President, Grand Master or

President, and the Grand Lodge or Rebekah Assembly. Decisions of the Grand Lodge or Rebekah Assembly may be appealed to the Sovereign Grand Master and The Sovereign Grand Lodge or to the President and the IARA.

4

RUNNING A LODGE

Overview

Running a lodge is fundamentally not so different from running any other type of organization. One thing to bear in mind is that unlike a business, everyone who participates in a lodge is a volunteer and doesn't need to be there. If they have a good experience they will come back and perhaps even get more involved. If they don't, you may never see them again.

Sharing power and responsibility is very important in a lodge organization. Individuals generally will not feel invested in a group unless they have some say in the decisions of that group.

Lodges which are run by a single individual, regardless of what office that individual may occupy are never as strong as lodges with a dedicated core of active members. It is not realistic to expect every lodge member to take initiative and to be engaged, but the more members who are given the room to grow into leaders, the more dynamic and effective a lodge will be.

While everyone has different needs and abilities, it is also critical to have a common core of values and principles. The fundamental principles of Odd Fellowship are a part of the glue that ties a lodge together, but they must be supplemented with a shared understanding of what these principles mean and how they can be implemented in practice.

Drafting a mission statement for your lodge, or even just holding periodic discussions of what the values and goals of the lodge are, can serve to get everyone on the same page.

Meetings

Meetings are the way an organization brings together a group of people in order to accomplish tasks. They are not an end unto themselves. Our real ends are the principles and goals of the Order and of the individual lodges. Odd Fellow and Rebekah lodges use meetings as a way to further these goals.

Meetings should be efficient and not waste undue amounts of the members' time. Their time is valuable and by treating it as such, we demonstrate our respect for our brothers and sisters in the Order. There are many tricks a good leader can use to keep a meeting on track.

Preparing in advance is essential. This can include reviewing the correspondences to determine which ones need to be read and which ones do not. It can include ensuring that all bills to be paid arrive on the Secretary's desk with ample time for warrants to be drawn and for the Finance Committee to inspect before the meeting begins. It can also include familiarizing the appropriate officers with complicated procedures they need to perform in advance, such as balloting on a new member—one of the most complex tasks a Warden ever needs to perform in the lodge.

Managing the flow of debate is also a vital function of the chairperson of a meeting. A member should not be allowed to speak more than twice on any particular issue unless further input from them is of great importance to the decision being made. No discussion should be allowed unless there is a motion on the floor. If the lodge is continuing to discuss an issue on which there appears to be general consensus, the chair should encourage the lodge to consider ending discussion and going straight to a vote.

The atmosphere of a meeting is also critical to success. A meeting should not be so overly formal and rigid that no one dares to smile, let alone laugh. Neither should it be so loose and unstructured that no one present retains any respect for the lodge and its work. The best meetings are relaxed and warm. Everyone feels safe expressing their views and sharing in the occasional joke with their brothers and sisters. After the meeting no one wants to go home right away, but remains afterwards, perhaps consuming some refreshments and basking in the glow of fraternity with their fellow members.

Committees

One of the best ways to organize the work of the lodge and keep it moving along briskly is through the appropriate use of committees. A committee could be a permanent ("standing") committee such as a Finance Committee, a Building Committee, or a Membership Committee. There are also ad hoc committees established for shorter term purposes such as a By-Law Committee for revising the by-laws or even a committee established just for one event, such as an annual holiday party.

Committees are generally appointed by the presiding officer who is automatically an ex-officio member of all committees. No complicated decision should ever come before the lodge until it's been through a committee.

Committees are designed to meet in between lodge meetings so that a small group of lodge members who have, or are willing to take, a particular interest in the matter at hand and report back to the lodge on what they have learned and what they recommend. This saves the lodge the time and trouble of hashing out all the details on the floor.

In addition to keeping meetings running smoothly, committees are also a great way to engage the members of the lodge so everyone has a role to play. A wise leader will establish a new committee to research and help settle an issue when they see that a discussion on the floor of the lodge is going on overly long and perhaps beginning to try the patience of the brothers and sisters assembled.

Finances

Financial procedures allow for transparency. They provide a system of checks and balances so that the lodge members may be satisfied that their money is well protected. There are some minor variations in the exact procedures followed from lodge to lodge but certain commonalities reign.

Incoming payments go to the Financial Secretary who records them in a receipts ledger. Payment of dues or assessments is further recorded in a member's account so it is possible to know which members are "in good standing." All funds are turned over to the Treasurer for deposit and to be recorded in the Treasurer's financial books.

Bills initially go to either the Secretary or the Finance Committee, depending on who writes the warrants for bill payment in that lodge. The bills are reviewed and if approved, the warrants are signed by the Finance Committee. The warrants are also to be signed by the Noble Grand.

At the appropriate point in the meeting, the Finance Committee makes a recommendation to the lodge as to whether or not the bills be paid, after which the lodge votes on the matter. The bills may not be paid until the Finance Committee has examined and signed them and the lodge has voted. This ensures that no unscrupulous member of the lodge can unilaterally issue a check. Many lodges add a further level of protection by requiring two signatures on all checks. The Treasurer makes out the checks and records the expense in their books.

Best practice also includes periodic reconciling of the Treasurer's books against the actual bank account. Even the most honest and diligent of officers will occasionally make a mathematical or other error and reconciling with the bank statements will allow this to be rectified. This also allows for verification that no money is being spent without going through the proper lodge channels.

The Finance Committee typically conducts an annual audit of the books at the end of the year in preparation for filing the annual report. The financial books must also be made available to the District Deputy Grand Master, District Deputy President, or any other officer designated by the Grand Master or President to audit the books of the lodge.

Events

Planning events is a big part of what an active lodge does. Events can fall in a variety of different types. Which ones are most prevalent will depend on the interests and taste of the individual lodge. Most successful lodges will have a variety of different types of events including social functions, service or charitable events, and degree work. Some of these can also be opportunities to engage with the broader community and get more publicity for your lodge.

Lodges typically have certain tried-and-true social events that they hold year after year, such as a "Roll Call Dinner" in which the names and length of membership of each lodge member is read aloud. Common social events also include barbecues, potlucks, speakers, outings, concerts, or holiday parties. There really is no limit to the options available so long as the event doesn't violate the values or principles of our Order. A number of lodges have doubled down on the word "odd" and successfully organized some very creative or off-beat social events.

A lodge should take great care to ensure there are at least some events which interest each of their different types of members. When new members join, it's often a good idea to find out what sorts of events those members would like to have and try some new events with them in mind. Ideally, the new members will even get involved in organizing some of the new events themselves.

Which service or charity events are appropriate for a lodge depends on the composition of the lodge as well as the community around it. A lodge with a smaller number of members or with members who are less able to do physical work should look into opportunities appropriate to the number of members and their abilities. It's generally a better idea to get involved in something hands-on than to just write a check, because it gives the members a feeling of achievement and satisfaction to accomplish good with their own hands. Working together for the common good can also strengthen the bonds of friendship and fraternity within the lodge. If you are not sure what the needs of your local community are, you could consider contacting a local homeless shelter or other nonprofit to find out what their needs are and how you can be of service.

Degree work is very special in that it's the time when we pass on the meaning of what it is to be an Odd Fellow or Rebekah to the next generation. Not every lodge is able to organize their own degree team, but for those who can, the conferring of degrees can be a very moving experience when done properly. When a member initially receives a degree, they have many impressions and feelings regarding what they have just seen, but they rarely understand the full depth of the degree. It is only after repeated viewings, or better yet, actually performing a part in the degree oneself that the full flower of its meaning can bloom.

Degree work should be performed with care and seriousness. There needs to be a level of respect for the degree or the candidates will very easily pick up on the fact that it doesn't mean much to the members who are conferring it. Practice is very important here because even if one reads from the book, it is still possible to tell who has cared enough to practice and who has not. If you read from the book, be sure to practice enough that you can read and pronounce the words fluently. One you can read it fluently, you can think about what it means and then you can read it with real depth of feeling. Likewise, it is important to practice the floorwork so that you can move around the room deliberately and without confusion.

While we must have respect for the Ritual, we must also have respect for the candidates. They may have never undergone any sort of ritual initiation and it may be a new and overwhelming experience for them. It is important that the candidates be made to feel comfortable in every possible way during degree work. If they seem confused or anxious they should be guided or reassured. It's okay, to go a little bit off script if it helps a candidate to better understand what is happening or to feel secure enough to fully engage with the material being presented.

For any type of event, including social events, service events and degree work, if you belong to a smaller lodge you may wish to consider combining with other lodges or even your entire district to bolster your capabilities. We are always stronger when we work together with each other.

5

HOW TO GROW MEMBERSHIP

If the lodges in your district are all doing the things described above then you are already well on your way to building membership.

The first step is always making our lodges inviting places where people will want to spend their time. If a lodge is unpleasant or boring then all the promotional efforts and recruiting in the world will be for naught. What good is it to bring members in the door only to have them head straight for the exit?

That being said, once you've made your lodges into spaces where new members might want to spend some time, the next step is getting the word out. A lot of recruiting happens organically in a well-functioning lodge. If a member is having a great time and going to engaging events, they can't help but want to share it with their friends. Bringing someone along to a public event may be all it takes to get a new member.

How you explain Odd Fellowship and your lodge to a person should depend on their own interests and background. Odd Fellowship has many different aspects to it and there are many different types of people in the world. It is best to focus on the aspects of the lodge which would most of interest to your audience, though you must also be forthright and honest about any aspect of the lodge which they may not like so as to avoid any surprises later. There is obviously something you like about your lodge or you wouldn't continue to be involved, so if you can articulate that to others, they will probably want to join as well.

The greatest challenge is often in bringing in people who are different than one's self. To truly have a vibrant lodge and to fulfill our aspiration of uniting all men and women of the world together in harmony and fraternity it is essential to also be able to bring in people who are different from you. Do your best to put yourself in their position. What is important to them? What do they like to do for fun? How could your lodge help them to improve and elevate themselves? Odd Fellowship is a big enough tent for everyone and if you look carefully you can find a place where they might fit.

One strategy that lodges around the country have been successful with and which is especially helpful for a smaller lodge seeking to grow is to find non-profit organizations with compatible goals and interests to our own and to work together with them on their projects. These organizations can be a source of individuals who are already civically-minded and may make excellent members. When you offer them the use of your hall for their events and spend some time getting to know their members it is often only natural that some of them will want to unite with you. Once you have individuals with several different types of interests, whether they be hobbies, professional interests, service work, performance, or anything else, you are well on your way to having a diverse lodge capable of attracting a wide variety of different types of members.

6

CONCLUSION

We hope the foregoing materials have been helpful to you in your quest to be a great District Deputy Grand Master or District Deputy President and a better Odd Fellow or Rebekah. There are many other resources you can turn to in order to serve the Order through your term and beyond.

You should familiarize yourself with the Ritual, the codes, and the various printed instruction booklets provided for members of our Order. Perhaps more importantly, though, never be afraid to ask for help. Within the Order, there are many who have been around for a long time, served in many offices, and have had many experiences you haven't yet had. Take all the opportunities you can to learn from your brothers and sisters. We wish you a great year and much success in your current role!

www.ingramcontent.com/pod-product-compliance
Lightning Source LLC
Chambersburg PA
CBHW061327120626
46546CB00007B/2715